Is It An Alligator or A Crocodile?

Animal Book 6 Year Old Children's Animal Books

BABY PROFESSOR

EDUCATION KIDS

Speedy Publishing LLC

40 E. Main St. #1156

Newark, DE 19711

www.speedypublishing.com

Copyright 2017

In this book, we're going to talk about the differences between alligators and crocodiles. So, let's get right to it!

THE EVOLUTION OF CROCODILIANS

The ancestors to the birds and crocodiles that we know today are the same group of animals that gave rise to dinosaurs. These common ancestors, called the archosaurs, lived 240 million years ago.

After the dinosaurs went extinct about 65 million years ago, birds evolved very rapidly, but the evolution of crocodiles has moved very, very slowly. Crocodilians is the name of the group of animals that includes the crocodiles as well as the alligators we have on Earth today.

In contrast to birds, crocodiles and alligators have not changed much from their prehistoric forms. By studying their body shapes, scientists have discovered that in prehistoric times, these animals ran like dogs on land to get away from meat-eating dinosaurs.

Instead of evolving from an animal that lived in the water and then moved to land, with crocodiles and alligators it was the other way around. They lived first on land and then took to the water to survive. After the asteroid hit the Earth and the dinosaurs started to die out, crocodiles took to the seas and their jaws evolved to catch fast prey like fish.

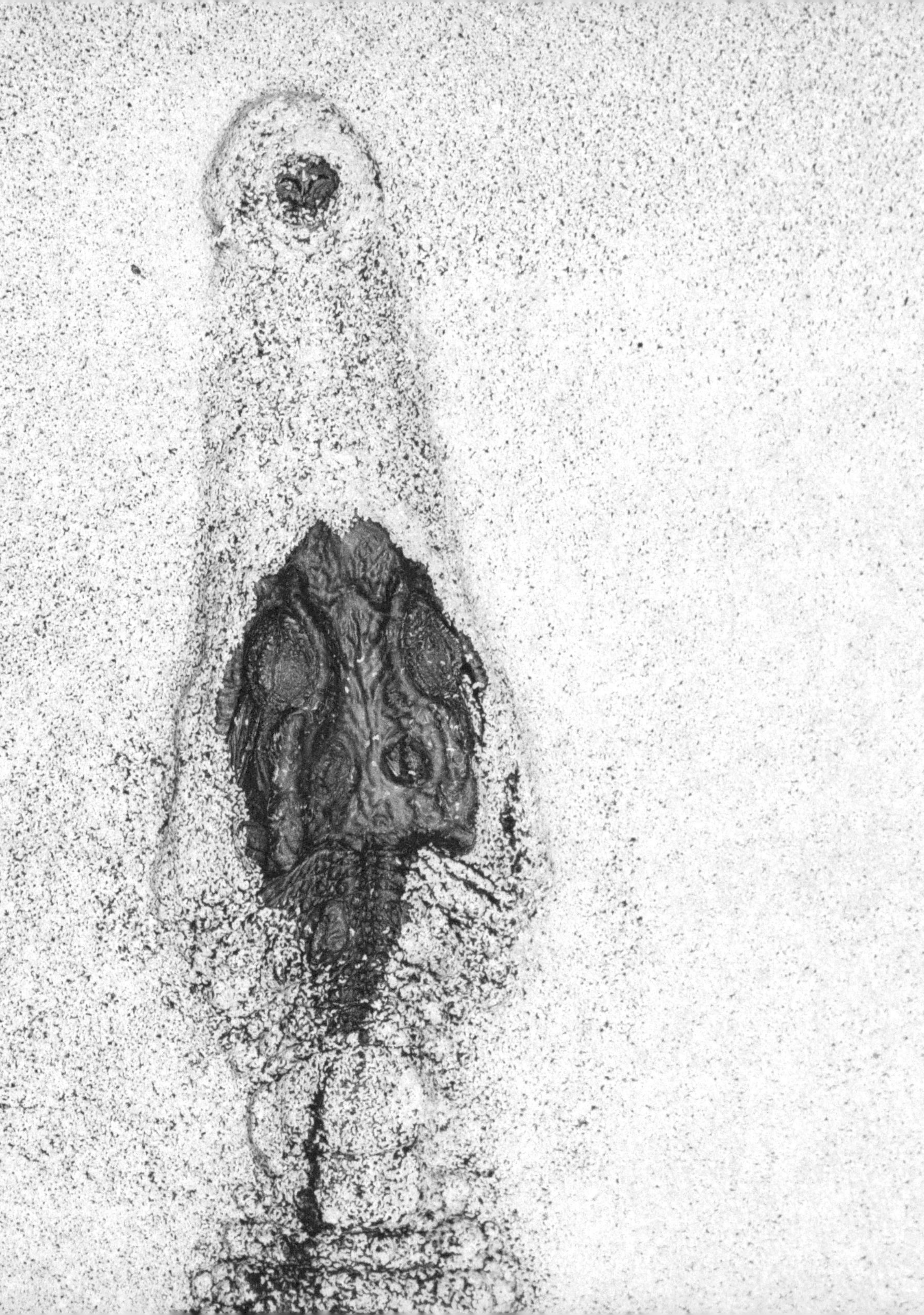

ALLIGATORS AND CROCODILES

Both alligators and crocodiles are cold-blooded reptiles. Both types of animals are carnivores, which simply means they eat meat. Alligators and crocodiles both have nicknames. Alligators are sometimes just called gators and crocodiles are just called crocs. They look alike until you get to know more about them. Then you can easily tell them apart.

WHAT IS THE DIFFERENCE BETWEEN THE TWO?

Some of the differences between alligators and crocodiles are: their snout shape and teeth, the color of their skin and the location of their sensor pits, how they build their nests, and their habitats, which are just the places they live.

SNOUT SHAPE AND TEETH

One way to tell them apart is that an alligator has a very wide head and a snout that's shaped like the letter "U." A crocodile has a narrow head and kind of a long snout shaped like the letter "V." When an alligator's mouth is closed, only its top teeth can be seen. On the other hand, when a crocodile's mouth is shut tight, you can still see both its top and bottom teeth.

COLOR OF SKIN AND SENSOR PITS

Another way you can tell the difference is that alligators are dark gray or black in color. Crocodiles are kind of tan-colored or have greenish-gray skin. Alligators have sensor pits only on their heads, while crocodiles have them all over their bodies. These sensor pits are bumps in their skin that are even more sensitive than human fingertips! Both alligators and crocodiles have dry, hard scales on their bodies.

NEST BUILDING

Both gators and crocs lay eggs, but they build different kinds of nests. Alligators build their nests above ground and lay about 45 eggs. On the other hand, crocodiles build their nests underground and lay about 50 eggs.

HABITATS

Alligators live in North America as well as eastern China. American crocodiles live in North America in a very small area of southern Florida. They also live in southern Mexico, Central America, the Caribbean, and the northern regions of South America. The American crocodile is an endangered species. Different species of crocs live in Africa, Australia, and Asia.

FRESH WATER VERSUS SALT WATER

Alligators only live in habitats with freshwater. Some types of crocodiles live in freshwater habits and some live in saltwater.

HOW FAST ARE THEY?

It's true that both alligators and crocodiles can rest in the sun for hours and be very, very still. They almost look like they are dead, they move so little. However, don't get too close. If they wake up, they can move very fast when they sprint short distances. They definitely can outrun people. It's never a good idea to get too close to a gator or croc.

HOW BIG DO THEY GET?

Gators and crocs are big reptiles. An alligator can grow to 19 feet long from head to tip of tail. Crocs get even bigger at 28 feet long.

WHAT DO THEY EAT?

Both these types of big reptiles are meat-eaters. They hunt down and kill anything they can. Fish and amphibians, such as frogs are part of their diet. So are birds and deer depending on where their native habitat is. They have sharp teeth, however they use them for tearing not for chewing. They swallow torn off meat in whole chunks. Although carnivores are usually strictly meat-eaters, alligators will eat fruit.

TYPES OF ALLIGATORS

There are only two types of alligators- American alligators and Chinese alligators.

The American alligator is found in the states of Florida and Louisiana in the United States. The Chinese alligator is only found in the swamps and ponds of the Yangtze River in the country of China. Unfortunately, the Chinese alligator is endangered because the place where these creatures live is getting polluted and too filled with people for the alligators to survive. Rice farmers in China kill the alligators because they destroy the farmers' rice paddies.

Alligators often group together as they swim or stay out in the sun. A group of alligators is called a congregation.

Chinese alligators are much smaller than American alligators, which reach an average length of about 15 feet and weigh up to 1,000 pounds.

TYPES OF CROCODILES

There are three types of crocodiles-American crocodiles, Nile crocodiles, and Saltwater crocodiles.

AMERICAN CROCODILE

The American crocodile is an endangered species. Its habitats in the Americas are shrinking. It's one of the largest types of crocodiles worldwide, getting to 20 feet in length and up to 2,000 pounds in weight.

NILE CROCODILE

These 16-foot, 1,200 pound crocs live in the Nile River in Africa. They mainly eat fish, but they will hunt and attack anything that comes into their path including small hippos, porcupines, and zebras. Over 200 people die each year because they got too close to the jaws of a Nile crocodile.

SALTWATER CROCODILE

Saltwater crocodiles are very dangerous animals. A saltwater crocodile waits near the water's edge until its potential prey stops for a drink of water. Then, it explodes out, grasps its victim in its jaws, and drags it underwater until it drowns. Just like the Nile croc, Saltwater crocodiles will go after people. These scary reptiles get up to 23 feet long and up to 2,200 pounds in weight. They live in Southeast Asia and Northern Australia.

FASCINATING FACTS ABOUT ALLIGATORS AND CROCODILES

Warm temperatures make alligator eggs turn into males and cold temperatures make their eggs turn into females. The muscles in alligators' jaws are so weak that a person can hold them closed. Don't try this though, because they have a powerful bite!

Because they are cold-blooded, both alligators and crocodiles have to cool off by getting in the shade or swimming in the water. Like lizards and snakes, they warm up by sunbathing in the warmth of the sun.

Baby crocodiles like to ride on their mom's backs. A mother's mouth is a great place for a baby croc to hide if a predator is after it.

Mother gators and
mother crocs take
care of their babies
after they hatch in
the nest.

Both types of reptiles can stay underwater for an hour or more even though they need oxygen to live.

Both types of reptiles have excellent eyesight and hearing. Their sense of smell is sensitive as well. Even though they do well on land, both crocs and gators spend a lot of time in the water.

Another type of animal similar to gators and crocs is the caiman. Caimans are more closely related to alligators than crocodiles, even though their bodies are narrower than alligators.

Australians call their saltwater crocodiles "salties" for short.

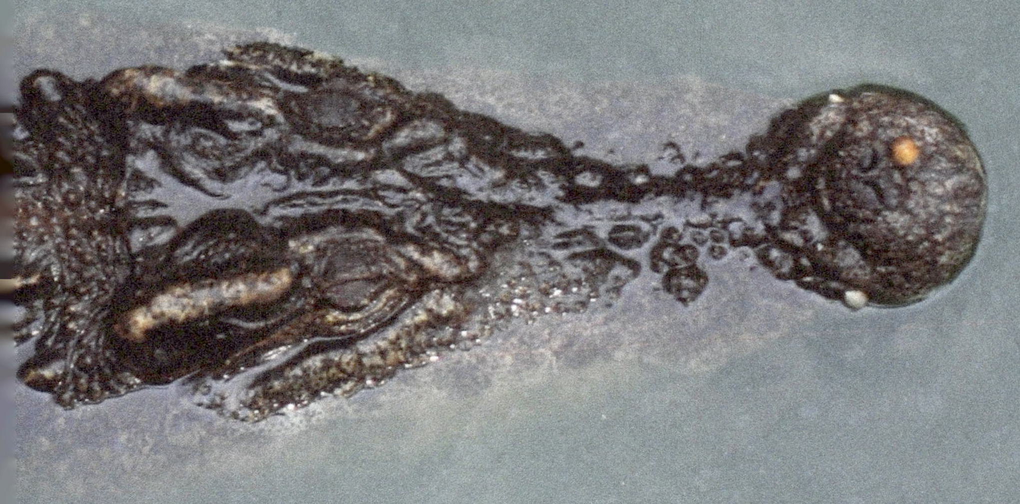

Both mummified crocodiles and mummified croc eggs have been found deep in-
side Egyptian tombs.

Alligators have one of the most powerful
bites ever recorded. They bite down with
almost 3,000 pounds of force.

The phrase "crying crocodile tears" means that you're crying fake tears. It came from the myth that these reptiles cry when eating people. Their eyes do froth when eating but they aren't crying.

A young alligator can eat over 20% of its body weight at one meal. That would be like an adult human eating over 40 pounds of steak in one sitting!

When a crocodile sits on a river bank, it opens its mouth. This is a way to cool off its temperature since it has sweat glands in its mouth.

About 7% of the time, baby alligators are killed by other alligators. Alligator blood combats bacteria, which means that even if an alligator loses its leg in fight, it usually doesn't get infected.

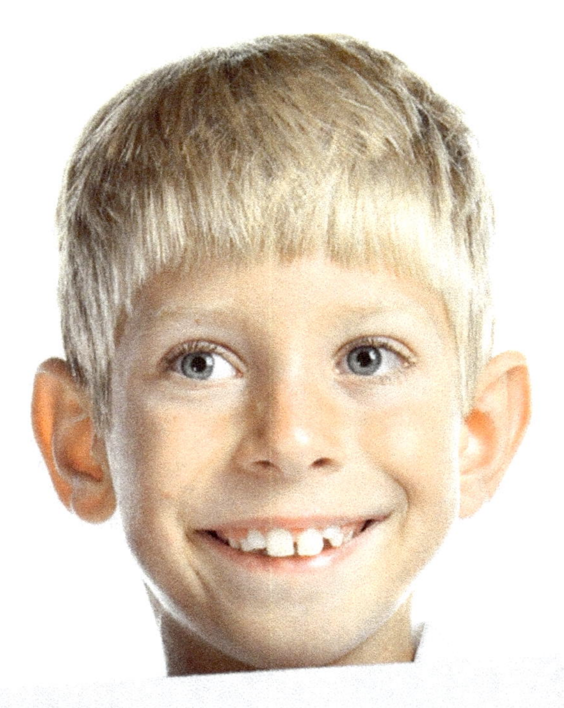
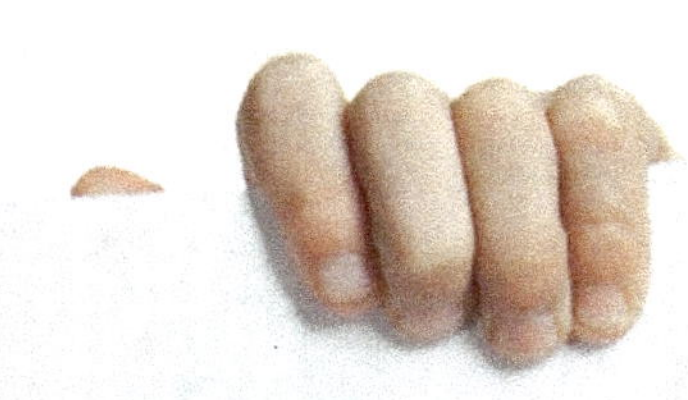
Awesome! Now you know more about alligators and crocodiles. You can find more Animal books from Baby Professor by searching the website of your favorite book retailer.

Visit

BABY PROFESSOR
EDUCATION KIDS

www.BabyProfessorBooks.com
to download Free Baby Professor eBooks
and view our catalog of new and exciting
Children's Books